THAT TIME I GOT REINCARNATED AS A
SLIME
16

Author: FUSE

Artist: TAIKI KAWAKAMI

Character design: MITZ VAH

World Map

ARMORED NATION
OF DWARGON

KINGDOM
OF FALMUTH

KINGDOM
OF BLUMUND

GREAT FOREST
OF JURA

SEALED CAVE

TEMPEST,
LAND OF MONSTERS

SORCEROUS
DYNASTY OF
THALION

ANIMAL
KINGDOM OF
EURAZANIA

PLOT SUMMARY

Rimuru completed his ascension to Demon Lord, and succeeded at saving the lives of Shion and the others killed in the attack. Diablo, the demon he summoned during the battle, becomes the newest resident of Tempest. But this does not mean normal life has returned. Disposing of the King of Falmuth, the existence of the Western Holy Church that intends to wipe out monster-kind, the activity of the sneaky Demon Lord Clayman... There is no end to Rimuru's problems. Then he hears from Raphael, the evolved version of Great Sage, that the deciphering of "Unlimited Imprisonment" is soon to be complete. ▼

 =

VELDORA TEMPEST
(Storm Dragon Veldora)

▷ Rimuru's friend and name-giver. A Catastrophe-class monster.

RIMURU TEMPEST
(Satoru Mikami)

▷ An otherworlder who was formerly human and was reincarnated as a slime. Now a Demon Lord.

SHIZUE IZAWA

▷ An otherworlder summoned from wartime Japan. Deceased.

RIGURD
▷ Goblin village chieftain.

GOBTA
▷ A ditzy goblin.

RANGA
▷ Tempest Star Wolf. Hides in Rimuru's shadow.

BENIMARU
▷ Kijin. Samurai general.

KINGDOM OF ENGRASSIA

SHUNA
▷ Kijin. Holy princess.

SHION
▷ Kijin. Samurai. Rimuru's bodyguard.

SOEI
▷ Kijin. Spy.

HAKURO
▷ Kijin. Instructor.

THE WESTERN NATIONS

TREYNI
▷ A dryad, protector of the great forest.

GABIRU
▷ Head warrior of the lizardmen.

GELD
▷ Orc King.

DIABLO
▷ A demon who serves Rimuru.

MILIM NAVA
▷ One of the Ten Great Demon Lords. Catastrophe-class threat. Childish.

YOUM
▷ Human. Champion. From the Kingdom of Falmuth.

MJURRAN
▷ Majin. Wizard. Under Clayman's control.

GRUCIUS
▷ Lycanthrope. Warrior of Eurazania.

CONTENTS

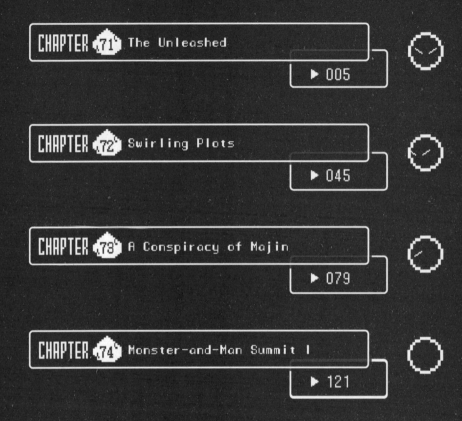
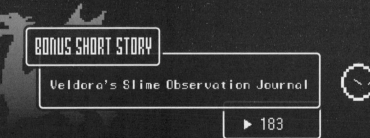

I'VE DECIDED TO BECOME A DEMON LORD IN BOTH NAME AND FACT.

LISTEN UP, EVERYONE.

BEFORE WE TALK ABOUT THE FUTURE, THERE'S ONE THING I'D LIKE TO MAKE CLEAR.

BUT YOU ALREADY *ARE*... RIGHT?

A PUBLIC AN-NOUNCEMENT...

MEANING, INTRODUCING YOURSELF TO THE TEN GREAT DEMON LORDS?

YES, THAT!

WELL, YEAH, I DID BECOME A *TRUE DEMON LORD*, AS THEY CALL IT.

BUT I HAVEN'T MADE A PUBLIC AN-NOUNCEMENT, HAVE I?

THERE'S ONE I'D LIKE TO CHALLENGE TO A FIGHT.

MAY I ASK THE REASON WHY?

HE'S ALSO USING MILIM TO WIPE OUT OUR ALLY, EURAZANIA.

DEMON LORD CLAYMAN.

WHILE WE WERE UNDER ATTACK, HE MANIPULATED MJURRAN IN ORDER TO MAXIMIZE THE DAMAGE.

I WON'T ALLOW HIM TO TOY WITH US ANY LONGER.

...BUT I CAN'T OVERLOOK WHAT HE'S DONE.

I DON'T KNOW WHY HE'S BEEN SNEAKING AROUND LIKE THIS...

CHAPTER 71: The Unleashed

I WILL STRIKE AGAINST DEMON LORD CLAYMAN.

ANY OBJECTIONS?

NONE AT ALL.

NONE HERE.

DO AS YOU WILL, MY LORD.

WE WILL FOLLOW YOU.

WE'VE GOT YOUR BACK!

YUP.

LET US HANDLE WHATEVER WEAPONS AND ARMOR YOU NEED.

SOEI...

MY LORD.

THAT'S WHAT I LIKE ABOUT SOEI. HE'S GOOD AT HIS JOB.

O-OKAY.

Didn't even say anything yet...

I WILL COLLECT INTELLI-GENCE ON CLAYMAN AT ONCE.

HUP

HUP

HUP

YES, SIR.

HUP

THANK YOU, SOEI.

WE'LL WAIT FOR THE INTELLI-GENCE TO COME IN BEFORE HOLDING A FULL TACTICAL MEETING.

...CHAN-CELLOR OF THE JURA FOREST.

WE WOULD BE HAPPY TO HELP...

BEAST-KETEERS, I WILL NEED YOUR HELP AS WELL.

...AND DEBTS WITH OUR LIVES.

LYCAN-THROPES REPAY TRUST WITH TRUST...

WE'RE IN YOUR DEBT FOR TAKING IN OUR REFUGEES.

YOU HAVE OUR FULL TRUST.

...WE OWE YOU MORE THAN WE CAN POSSIBLY OFFER.

IN BOTH PERSONAL TERMS, AND SPEAKING FOR OUR SPECIES AS A WHOLE...

...IN RECOMPENSE FOR WHAT YOU'VE DONE.

WE WOULD GIVE YOU OUR LIVES...

ORDER US AS YOU SEE FIT.

FOR NOW, REST AND BUILD YOUR STRENGTH FOR THE FIGHT TO COME.

YES, SIR!

THEN I WILL BE IN CHARGE OF YOUR LIVES UNTIL THE MOMENT I RETURN YOU TO CARRION.

ALL RIGHT...

NOW, LISTEN CLOSELY. ABOVE ALL ELSE, A PERSONAL SECRETARY...

...MUST EXIST FOR THE SAKE OF THE MASTER.

I SEE. THIS IS VERY HELPFUL.

WHAT IS SHION TELLING HIM...?

...TO DO WHAT HE NEEDS, EVEN IF HE HASN'T GIVEN THE COMMAND YET.

YOU MUST ALWAYS SENSE HIS MIND, AND BE READY...

AH!

WEREN'T YOU SUPPOSED TO BE FOLLOWING THOSE ORDERS LORD RIMURU GAVE YOU, SHION?

YOU OVER- HEARD OUR LITTLE PRE- MEETING?

YES. I PICKED IT UP WITH THOUGHT COMMUNI- CATION.

LORD RIMURU!

HEY, GABIRU.

14

YOU'RE AN OFFICER NOW. YOU WILL NEED TO ATTEND THE MEETINGS WHERE WE MAKE IMPORTANT DECISIONS.

I'VE DECIDED TO PUT YOU IN CHARGE OF THE DEVELOPMENT DIVISION.

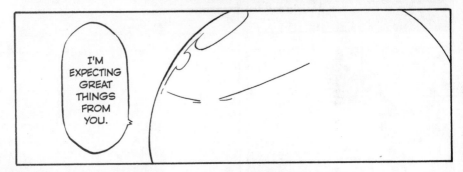

I'M EXPECTING GREAT THINGS FROM YOU.

YI...

H-HEY, STOP! DON'T CELEBRATE LIKE THAT!

Yea-hah!

YIPPEEEE!! MASTER GABIRU'S GOTTEN A PROMOTION!!

RAAH

I NEED TO DO SOMETHING IN THE DEEPEST PART OF THE CAVE.

MAKE SURE NO ONE ELSE APPROACH-ES.

Y-YES, SIR! OF COURSE!

Uh, really...?

YOU WERE ABOUT TO SAY "YIPPEE", TOO, WEREN'T YOU?

THESE ARE DIGNIFIED MOMENTS! YOU HAVE TO BE STOIC!

WHA—?!

You heard that?!

...BUT NOW I'M WORRIED HE'LL BE TOO EXCITED TO STAND WATCH AS CAREFULLY AS HE SHOULD.

POYO ぽよ POYO ぽよ

THE PROMOTION I'M GIVING HIM IS WELL-DESERVED...

GABIRU'S WORKED HARD FOR THIS.

CONGRATULATIONS, MASTER! GA-BI-RU! GA-BI-RU!

AFTER ALL...

POYO... ぽよ...

DESPITE HOW HE SEEMS, VELDORA IS KIND OF A GUARDIAN DEITY FOR THE GREAT FOREST OF JURA.

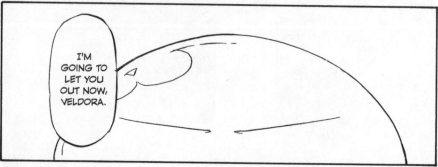

I'M GOING TO LET YOU OUT NOW, VELDORA.

RAPHAEL, UNDO "UNLIMITED IMPRISON-MENT."

DONE.

UGH. THIS GUY AND HIS INSISTENCE ON SPECIAL TREATMENT.

I'VE FINALLY RETURNED... AND THIS IS HOW YOU TREAT ME?

I'M A DEMON LORD NOW.

WELL, A LOT OF STUFF'S HAPPENED.

I HAD EXPECTED THIS DAY WOULD COME MUCH, MUCH LATER.

STILL, THIS IS HAPPENING SOONER THAN I ANTICIPATED.

AH, YOU DON'T SAY.

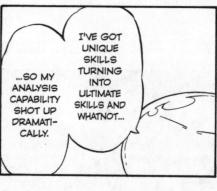

...SO MY ANALYSIS CAPABILITY SHOT UP DRAMATICALLY.

I'VE GOT UNIQUE SKILLS TURNING INTO ULTIMATE SKILLS AND WHATNOT...

24

YOU... DON'T SEEM VERY SURPRISED BY THIS.

W-WHAT?! NO, NO, I AM *VERY* STARTLED!!

THIS IS NEWS TO ME, BECAUSE I WAS NOT SPYING ON YOU!!

GASP

ANSWER: IT IS THE SAME THING AS A TRUE DEMON LORD.

AWAKENED DEMON LORD?

That was suspicious...

HOW IS IT POSSIBLE FOR ONE TO GROW SO QUICKLY?

SO, YOU HAVE BECOME AN AWAKENED DEMON LORD IN JUST TWO YEARS...

WELL, WHAT CAN I SAY? I GUESS I'M JUST A GENIUS?

WHEN I GAVE MY FRIENDS NAMES, THEY ALL EVOLVED AND STUFF.

YOU BLITHERING FOOL.

THE NAME IS DERIVED FROM THE PROCESS OF A DEMON LORD SEED UNDERGOING THE HARVEST FESTIVAL.

AH, I SEE.

AND IT WAS SO RUINOUS TO MY EFFICIENCY THAT I ASSUMED MY LIBERATION WOULD COME VASTLY LATER.

PING

JIGGLE

WHY DO YOU THINK YOU COULD TOSS OUT NAMES WITH NO CONSEQUENCES?

BECAUSE YOU TOOK ALL THE MAGICULES YOU LACKED FROM *ME*, THAT IS WHY!

HUH?

YOU KNOW, I ALWAYS THOUGHT IT WAS STRANGE HOW I COULD EVOLVE SO MANY OF THEM SO EASILY, AND WITH SO LITTLE RISK.

IT WAS QUITE TAXING.

HARRUMPH.

MEANING... THE WHOLE REASON I COULD "NAME" EVERYONE WAS BECAUSE OF VELDORA?

GRUMP

WE'VE BROKEN YOU OUT OF THE "UNLIMITED IMPRISONMENT." YOU CAN FORGIVE ME, RIGHT?

WELL, IT'S IN THE PAST NOW.

BETTER BE CAREFUL WITH NAMING FROM NOW ON.

SUCH AS... A CRIMURU PUFF.

OH.

I WILL FORGIVE YOU... IF YOU HAVE A PRESENT FOR ME.

A PRESENT?

I WOULD ASSUME THERE'S A CONNECTION TO VELDORA IN THERE SOMEWHERE, TOO.

HMM?

I COMPLETELY FORGOT. DID YOU NOT GET A SPECIAL "GIFT"?

I HEARD THAT EVERYONE IN MY SOUL LINEAGE WAS SUPPOSED TO GET ONE WHEN I TURN INTO A DEMON LORD.

FLASH

...WHY DON'T WE GO OUTSIDE?

WE COULD SIT AROUND HERE AND TALK, IF YOU WANT. BUT SINCE YOU'RE BACK NOW...

FWOOO

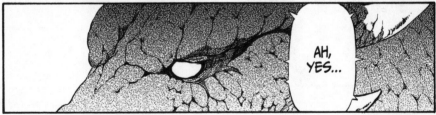

AH, YES...

I THINK WE CAN FIGURE SOMETHING OUT.

THEN WHAT SHALL BE DONE ABOUT MY FLESH?

IN OTHER WORDS, THIS IS JUST HIS SOUL.

RIGHT NOW, VELDORA IS A BEING OF PURE THOUGHT.

NORMALLY, SPIRITUAL BEINGS FROM THE ASTRAL REALM LIKE ELEMENTALS, DEMONS, AND DRAGONS DO NOT POSSESS PHYSICAL BODIES.

SPIRITUAL BEING

DEMON

SPIRIT

IN ORDER FOR THEM TO MANIFEST IN THE PHYSICAL REALM, THEY MUST INHABIT A VESSEL.

VESSEL

GOLEM

HUMAN GIRL

ARCH GOLEM

MAJIN

STABILIZED VIA PHYSICAL FORM

NEO VELDORA

ALTHOUGH THAT ENERGY WILL EVENTUALLY COALESCE INTO BEING AGAIN SOMEWHERE ELSE...

VEL-DORA!

...UNTIL IT VANISHES.

IF A SPIRITUAL BEING CONTINUES TO EXIST IN THE PHYSICAL REALM WITHOUT A MATERIAL BODY, ITS ENERGY STEADILY DISPERSES...

VEL-DORA! THERE YOU ARE!

EVEN IF THAT BEING WERE A STORM DRAGON BY THE NAME OF VELDORA...

...THE SPIRITUAL BEING'S MEMORY WILL BE SPOTTY.

...HE WOULD NO LONGER BE VELDORA, MY CLOSEST COMPANION.

WHAT DOES A SLIME WANT WITH ME?

AH... RIMURU? WAS THAT IT?

AT LEAST, ACCORDING TO THE EXPLANATION FROM THE WISE RAPHAEL.

YOU HAD A MATERIAL BODY BEFORE I DEVOURED YOU, RIGHT?

BUT IN YOUR STOMACH, I DID NOT NEED IT, SO I REUSED THE MAGICAL ENERGY.

YES, A BODY BUILT OF MAGICULES.

Ohh..

...

THERE ARE HUMANS IN TOWN, AND SOME WEAKER MONSTERS, AS WELL.

I WANT YOU TO SUPPRESS YOUR MASSIVE AURA.

WHAT IS THAT?

CAN YOU MAKE ME A PROMISE?

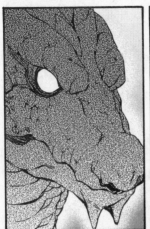

AH... I SEE. VERY WELL, I PROMISE.

GREAT. THANKS.

YOU HAVE TRULY BECOME A LORD.

RIMURU.

I GUESS.

IT'S A BODY DOUBLE.

ANOTHER RIMURU HAS EMERGED!

YOU CAN TELL, HUH?

AH. BUT AN AUGMENTED DOUBLE, AFTER EVOLUTION.

OHO...

USE IT AS YOUR VESSEL.

HEH.

HMM. YES.

IT IS
A GOOD
VESSEL.
I WILL USE
IT WITH
GRATITUDE.

KWA
HA
HA
HA
HA
!

NOTICE: THERE IS AN IMPORTANT ANNOUNCEMENT.

WHAT?

AS A RESULT OF ANALYZING THE LAST VESTIGES OF VELDORA...

A "SOUL CORRIDOR" HAS BEEN CONFIRMED BETWEEN MASTER AND THE INDIVIDUAL VELDORA.

...YOU HAVE GAINED THE ULTIMATE SKILL "VELDORA," LORD OF STORMS.

ULTIMATE SKILL...?

WHAT? "VEL-DORA"?!

KWAA HA HA HA HA! I AM FULLY RESTORED!!

STOMP

TO THINK THE DAY WOULD COME SO QUICKLY WHEN WE CAN STARE EACH OTHER IN THE FACE AGAIN!

YOU HAVE MY THANKS, RIMURU!

GRAB

IT WAS THE RIGHT DECISION TO MAKE YOU MY BOSOM BUDDY.

THAT WAS SOMETHING I READ IN A MANGA FROM YOUR MEMORY. I WAS VERY BORED WITH NOT MUCH TO DO IN THERE!

ARE YOU SERIOUS, OLD MAN?!

BY THE WAY, VELDORA...

...WHERE DID YOU HEAR THAT LINE?

"All who defy me"...

AH, THAT?

...BUT FIRST LET'S ENJOY OUR REUNION.

I'M REALLY CURIOUS ABOUT THAT ULTIMATE SKILL...

HOW'S THIS ?!

Now you're just showing off.

MEETING AGAIN AFTER TWO YEARS TIME...

...FELT VERY MUCH THE SAME AS WHEN WE FIRST MET.

AND THAT MEANT ...

...I HAD NO IDEA THAT THE TOWN WAS IN AN ABSOLUTE PANIC DUE TO THE OVERWHELMING POWER OF VELDORA'S PRESENCE.

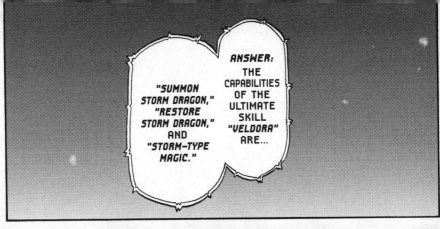

ANSWER: THE CAPABILITIES OF THE ULTIMATE SKILL *"VELDORA"* ARE...

"SUMMON STORM DRAGON," "RESTORE STORM DRAGON," AND *"STORM-TYPE MAGIC."*

ANSWER: VIA THE ESTABLISHMENT OF THE SOUL CORRIDOR, YOU CONTAIN A REPLICA OF THE INDIVIDUAL VELDORA'S MEMORY.

VELDORA'S SOUL

RIMURU'S SOUL

PRACTICING STIFLING HIS AURA

HAAAAAA

"SUMMON STORM DRAGON" AND *"STORM-TYPE MAGIC"* MAKE SENSE TO ME, I GUESS.

BUT WHAT'S *"RESTORE"* ?

YOU GOTTA HOLD IT IN MORE.

SO I GUESS VELDORA'S USING ME AS A BACKUP DRIVE, THEN.

THEREFORE, IF VELDORA SHOULD DIE FOR ANY REASON, AS THE MASTER, YOU CAN RECONSTRUCT HIS BODY.

CHAPTER 72 Swirling Plots

AND NOW, FOR THE FINISHING TOUCHES!

WE'RE ALMOST THERE.

HEY, YOU'RE GETTING PRETTY GOOD AT SUPPRESSING YOUR AURA.

SHALL I PROCESS THEM AND UPGRADE YOUR POWERS WHERE POSSIBLE?

YOU HAVE RECEIVED A GREAT NUMBER OF SKILLS IN TRIBUTE VIA *"FOOD CHAIN."*

YEAH. THANKS FOR HANDLING THAT, RAPHAEL.

THAT "FOOD CHAIN"...

NOTICE: EVOLUTION OF THE MONSTERS IN YOUR LINEAGE IS COMPLETE.

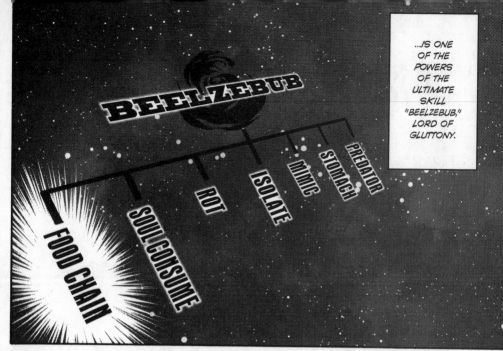

BEELZEBUB

FOOD CHAIN

SOUL CONSUME

ROT

ISOLATE

MIMIC

STOMACH

PREDATOR

...IS ONE OF THE POWERS OF THE ULTIMATE SKILL "BEELZEBUB," LORD OF GLUTTONY.

THE SKILLS OF THE MONSTERS WITHIN MY SOUL LINEAGE ARE CONCENTRATED INTO ME...

...AND A PART OF MY POWER IS GRANTED TO THEM IN RETURN.

NOTICE: COMBINATION AND DISPOSAL OF SKILLS COMPLETE.

OOH! THAT WAS FAST.

I DOUBT THAT RECEIVING A BUNDLE OF THEM AT ONCE MEANS I'LL BE ANY GOOD AT USING THEM.

NORMALLY, YOU'RE SUPPOSED TO GAIN SKILLS AFTER MUCH SELF-IMPROVEMENT AND EFFORT.

UNIQUE SKILL "UNLIMITED IMPRISON-MENT"...

...HAS EVOLVED INTO ULTIMATE SKILL "URIEL," LORD OF VOWS.

UM...

PHEW

DING!
ピ

Oh.

YES.

WEREN'T YOU JUST COMBINING REDUNDANT SKILLS AND DISCARDING INFERIOR ONES?!

HOLD ON.

HOLD ON JUST ONE SECOND!

JUST LIKE THAT?!

So casual...

AFFIRMATIVE. IT WAS ACQUIRED UPON FINAL ANALYSIS.

AND WASN'T UNLIMITED IMPRISONMENT THE ABILITY THE HERO USED TO LOCK UP VELDORA?!

You're scaring me, Raphael.

IS IT REALLY SUPPOSED TO BE THIS EASY TO GET ULTIMATE SKILLS?

OH...

"UNLIMITED IMPRISONMENT" WAS USED AS THE BASIS FOR THE COMBINATION AND DISPOSAL OF SKILLS.

CHOP
CHOP

AFFIRMATIVE. ITS POWERS ARE "UNLIMITED IMPRISONMENT," "CONTROL LAWS," "UNIVERSAL BARRIER," AND "DOMINATE SPACE."

WHAT DID YOU CALL IT? "URIEL"?

SO I GUESS I'M ABLE TO LOCK UP VELDORA, IF I WANT.

URIEL... AN ULTIMATE SKILL BORN FROM EVERYONE'S SKILLS.

THIS POWER IS PROOF OF THE BOND THAT TIES ME TO THEM.

STRENGTH, AND TREMENDOUS SECURITY.

HAVE YOU CONFIRMED ALL OF YOUR SKILLS, RIMURU?

SHUNK

AND HERE'S THE OTHER SOURCE OF THAT STRENGTH AND SECURITY.

YEAH.

SUCH A TASK IS NO CHALLENGE FOR ME AT ALL!

KWA HA HA HA HA!

YOU'VE LEARNED HOW TO CONTROL YOUR AURA, I SEE.

OUTTA THE WAY!

NO, IT'S FINE. I JUST WANT YOU TO GIVE BACK THE FEELING OF WONDER I WASTED.

WHAT? IS THAT BAD?

THAT'S RIGHT, PEOPLE OF EURAZANIA!

HE *ORDERED* ME NOT TO LET ANYONE APPROACH!

LORD RIMURU STATED THAT HE WOULD NOT NEED ACCOMPANIMENT.

I MUST REFUSE.

WHAT'S THIS ABOUT?

BUT IT'S BEEN THREE DAYS ALREADY!!

WE MUST NOT INTERRUPT HIM.

HE HAS HIS REASONS FOR STAYING IN THE CAVE.

THE LEGENDARY STORM DRAGON HAS RETURNED, HASN'T IT?!

ARE YOU REALLY JUST GOING TO SIT HERE TWIDDLING YOUR THUMBS WHILE YOUR MASTER MIGHT BE IN DANGER?!

THAT'S NOT KEEPING THE PEACE!

ENOUGH, DIABLO!

IF YOU DO NOT HOLD YOUR TONGUE, I WILL TEAR IT OUT—

YOU ARE A VERY NOISY CAT.

THERE IS NO DOUBT THAT LORD RIMURU IS SAFE.

BUT IF VELDORA *HAS* RETURNED, THEN WE CANNOT AFFORD TO ACT RASHLY.

LEAVE THIS SITUATION TO US—

OH... SORRY, EVERY- ONE.

DIDN'T MEAN TO PUT YOU IN A TIGHT SPOT.

L....

LORD RIMURU!

...TO GOOD OL' VELDORA HIMSELF!

HE'S A BIT SHY, BUT HE WANTS TO BE FRIENDS, SO PLAY NICE!

I SIMPLY HAVE NOT MET MANY WHO COULD SURVIVE BEING IN MY PRESENCE, THAT IS ALL!

D-DON'T BE F-FOOLISH! I'M NOT THE LEAST BIT SHY!

WELL? INTRO- DUCE YOUR- SELF!

AHEM!

NOW THAT YOU CAN SUPPRESS YOUR AURA, EVERYONE SEEMS SKEPTICAL THAT IT'S REALLY YOU.

If Lord Rimuru says so...

MURMUR

But he's not a dragon...

MURMUR

Is he really...?

HMM.

I SUPPOSE YOU MIGHT BE RIGHT.

NOD

NOD

THEN I SHALL TELL YOU!

DO YOU WANT TO KNOW?! I BET YOU DO!!

YOU MUST BE CURIOUS AS TO THE RELATIONSHIP BETWEEN MYSELF AND YOUR MASTER, RIMURU!

I AM THE STORM DRAGON, VELDORA TEMPEST!

WE'RE PALS!!

BAM!!

PALS!! LORD RIMURU AND LORD VELDORA ARE PALS!!

WOWWW!

STOP IT.

PALS!!

NOW I'M GETTING EMBARRASSED.

PALS!!

JABBER!

AH, YOU MUST BE THE DRYADS.

OUR GUARDIAN, MASTER VELDORA.

I CONGRATULATE YOU MOST WARMLY ON YOUR RETURN.

YOU TOOK US IN AFTER WE WERE BANISHED BY THE SPIRIT QUEEN.

WE OWE YOU MORE THAN WE CAN EVER REPAY.

HOW LONG IT'S BEEN! THANK YOU FOR MANAGING MY FOREST!

WE ARE NOT WORTHY OF THIS PRAISE.

THAT'S RIGHT, THEY WERE ORIGINALLY WITH RAMIRIS, HUH?

KWAAA HA HA HA!

RIMURU ALSO HELPED ME PRACTICE HOLDING IN MY CONSIDERABLE AURA!

Ahh.

HE PRACTICED HOLDING IN HIS AURA...

AND... WHAT IS THIS FORM YOU TAKE?

OH, THIS? IT IS A VESSEL RIMURU PROVIDED ME.

! KREEE!

I WANT TO ASK HOW TO BE FRIENDS WITH THE STORM DRAGON.

Is this guy ever *not* impressed?

I MUST ASK HIM HOW TO DO THIS LATER.

ANOTHER BRILLIANT IDEA FROM LORD RIMURU.

I HAVE RETURNED, LORD RIMURU.

SENSING

SOMETHING BIG HAS HAPPENED.

YOU LOOK SO COOL, LORD VELDORA!

RAAAH

RAAAH

I HAVE NEWS OF CLAYMAN'S ACTIVITIES...

SOEI!

CHATTER

CHATTER

YAMMER YAMMER

LET'S HEAR THE RESULTS OF YOUR INVESTIGATION IN THE MEETING ROOM.

ACTUALLY, I'D REALLY LIKE TO TAKE THE FOCUS OFF OF THIS EMBARRASSMENT.

PSST

SHOULD I JUST TELL YOU LATER?

TWING

YES, SIR.

AND CALL YOUM AND KAVAL HERE, TOO, JUST FOR GOOD MEASURE.

SUMMON ALL OF THE OFFICERS WHO ARE NOT PRESENT TO THE ROOM.

YEAH. WE'RE PREPARING TO CHOOSE OUR NEXT COURSE OF ACTION.

DID SOMETHING HAPPEN?

RIMURU...

AND IS THERE ANYTHING I CAN DO?

THERE CERTAINLY IS.

RUMBLE
RUMBLE...

CRASH

DAMN
IT ALL!

WIPED OUT BY A SINGLE MEASLY MAJIN...

HOW FRAIL THESE HUMAN ARMIES ARE!

CRUNCH

DID THAT DEMON DEFLECT IT INTO THE SKY ON PURPOSE?!

ON TOP OF THAT, PIRONĒ WAS KILLED WHILE PERFORMING RECON.

REGARDLESS OF WHETHER HE REACHED AWAKENING OR NOT...

STILL, I DID MANAGE TO CONFIRM THAT THE MAJIN POSSESSED 20,000 HUMAN SOULS.

...MY OWN AWAKENING WAS A FAILURE.

I HAVE WASTED THE OPPORTUNITY THAT MY MASTER GAVE ME...

TAP TAP

68

DEMON LORD MILIM HAS DISPATCHED DEMON LORD CARRION.

THE ANIMAL KINGDOM OF EURAZANIA HAS FALLEN.

TOK

TOK

I SEE.

...BUT NOW I'VE GAINED POWER.

YES. THE FAILURE OF THE PLAN HURTS...

THE ABSOLUTE POWER OF MILIM NAVA.

WAIT, FREY.

ARE YOU REALLY GOING TO LEAVE THIS BLOOD-THIRSTY MILIM ON MY DOORSTEP?

THAT'S ALL I HAVE TO REPORT.

I'VE REPAID MY DEBT TO YOU.

YOU SEEM TO BE MISREADING THE SITUATION, FREY.

TAKE HER WITH YOU AND DEAL WITH HER.

WHY? I HAVE NO MORE OBLIGATION TO HELP YOU.

MILIM IS MY PUPPET NOW.

THOSE EYES OF YOURS, SAID TO BE THE MOST BEAUTIFUL OF ALL THE DEMON LORDS'...

...DID THEY NOT JUST BEAR WITNESS TO EURAZANIA BEING WIPED OFF THE MAP?

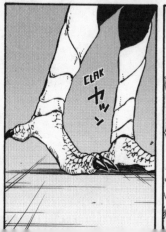

CLAK
カツン

YES... I SUPPOSE THAT WAS YOUR GOAL FROM THE START.

SEEING AS I'D RATHER NOT END UP LIKE CARRION JUST YET.

VERY WELL.

A WISE CHOICE, FREY.

YOU MAY GO.

I HAVE THE ACE UP MY SLEEVE NOW.

THERE IS NOTHING TO FEAR FROM THE OTHER DEMON LORDS ANYMORE.

...I CAN EASILY REAP THE SOULS OF THOUSANDS UPON THOUSANDS.

AND WITH MILIM'S POWER...

SFF

I WILL AWAKEN TO THE LEVEL OF TRUE DEMON LORD WITHOUT LIFTING A FINGER.

HEH HEH HEH HEH.

AT LAST, I CAN BE RID OF DEMON LORD LEON.

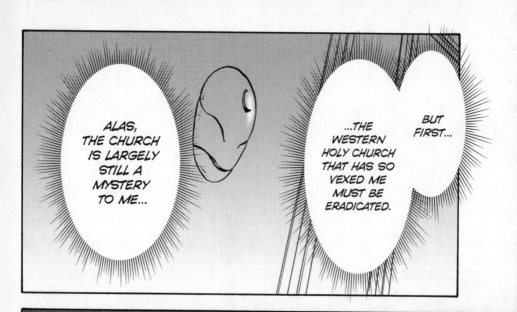

ALAS, THE CHURCH IS LARGELY STILL A MYSTERY TO ME...

...THE WESTERN HOLY CHURCH THAT HAS SO VEXED ME MUST BE ERADICATED.

BUT FIRST...

FOR NOW...

...I SHALL WAIT FOR LAPLACE TO RETURN FROM THE INFILTRATION MASTER ORDERED.

FLASH

WHAT TH' HELL WAS THAT FOR?!

THOUGHT THIS PLACE WAS S'POSED TO BE HOLY...

AAAAAH!!

SHWRR

HUP

THUD

So who could possibly have guessed...

OB-NOXIOUS LITTLE FLY...

The eradication of all monsters.

This is one of the tenets of Luminism, the religion of the Western Nations.

...that in the inner sanctum of this holy place...

CHAPTER 73 A Conspiracy of Majin

The Western Holy Church.

It began as a means to spread the religion of Luminism across the world...

...from its home of the Holy Empire of Lubelius.

At present, under the leadership of Hinata Sakaguchi, Captain of the Crusaders...

...it has gained vast influence, far beyond that of a mere subsidiary enterprise for Lubelius.

How-ever...

...it must still heed the commands of the mouthpiece of Luminus...

...the Holy Emperor of Lubelius.

Engrassia

C'mon, hurry!

HEY, wait up!

HA HA HA!

WHEW... THOUGHT I WAS A GONER THERE FOR SURE.

K-TUNK

WHO'RE YOU?

HMM?

KINDA FAMILIAR SOMEHOW, THOUGH...

WELL, IF SHE AIN'T A FINE-LOOKIN' LADY.

SPIN

YOUR MASTER AWAITS.

COME THIS WAY.

D-DID SHE JUST CALL ME AN IDIOT?

Heh.

YOU IDIOT.

LAPLACE OF THE MODERATE HARLEQUIN ALLIANCE, YES?

MY MASTER AWAITS, YOU SAY?

YOU EVEN KNOW WHO I AM?

HI THERE, LAPLACE.

I HEAR YOU'VE HAD A ROUGH TIME.

THE MASTER TOLD ME.

HAVE YOU DISCERNED THE TRUE NATURE OF THE WESTERN HOLY CHURCH, THEN?

OH...

THE SECURITY WAS SO TOUGH, I COULDN'T GET THROUGH!

GOSH, WHAT CAN I SAY...?

DID YOU AT LEAST CATCH A HINT?

MM-HMM.

AND?

...FOR GETTIN' STUCK IN YOUR PLOT WITHOUT REALIZIN' IT.

YA KNOW, I FEEL BAD FOR THAT SLIME...

YOU WOUND ME, SIR.

DARN...

I WAS HOPIN' THE DETAILS I WORKED SO HARD TA GLEAN WOULD FETCH ME A GOOD PRICE...

HA HA HA... WELL, YOU *ARE* A KNOWN LIAR.

SLUMP

SO MUCH FER THAT PLAN...

BUT YOU CAN'T BUTTER ME UP TO GET A HIGHER PAY RATE.

I'M HONORED BY THE COMPLIMENT.

WHAT?! YOU DO...?

YES. THE SOUL OF YOUR GROUP'S PRESIDENT, WHICH I'D BEEN KEEPING WITHIN MYSELF, HAS SAFELY ATTACHED TO ITS HOMUNCULUS...

HEY, DON'T SULK. AS A MATTER OF FACT, I ALREADY HAVE YOUR REWARD PREPARED FOR YOU.

THE PRESIDENT... AT LAST...

CALM DOWN.

HE'S BEEN HERE THE WHOLE TIME.

WHERE IS HE? LET ME SEE HIM!!

YOU MEAN THAT FINE-LOOKIN' LADY...?

HUH? BUT...

HANG ON...

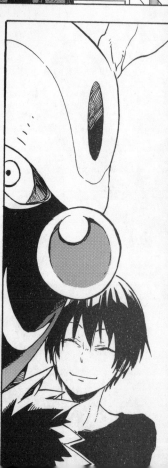

BWA HA HA HA HA HA !!

FLAP
FLAP

YOU REALLY WANTED A CHANGE IN STYLE, HUH?!

HEEEE HEE HEE!

WHY D'YA LOOK LIKE *THAT* ?!

IS THAT HOW YOU GREET YOUR PRESIDENT FOR THE FIRST TIME IN TWO HUNDRED YEARS?

SHUT UP, LAPLACE.

...BUT IT'S CERTAINLY DIFFERENT FROM THE OLD LOOK !!

I DUNNO IF I'D SAY IT *SUITS* YA...

BWA HA HA HA !

WELL, THAT WOULD EXPLAIN...

...WHY YA FELT SO FAMILIAR TO ME.

AFTER TEN YEARS OF WAITING, I FINALLY HAVE A BODY AGAIN.

I CAN PUT UP WITH A LITTLE INCONVENIENCE.

SNIK

I'VE AWAITED YOU, AND SO HAS FOOTMAN, AND TEAR...

...AND EVEN CLAYMAN.

WELCOME BACK, PRESIDENT KAZALIM.

THE MODERATE HARLEQUIN ALLIANCE HAS AWAITED YOUR RETURN.

WELL, I HATE TO POUR COLD WATER ON THIS TOUCHING REUNION, BUT...

...THIS ISN'T THE COMPLETE RETURN OF THE OLD DEMON LORD KAZALIM.

THAT CUR WILL PAY.

LEON CROMWELL...

CLENCH

MY STRENGTH IS NOT AS IT WAS DURING MY PRIME, I WILL ADMIT.

THAT IS TRUE.

THE HUMILIATION OF SUCH A DEFEAT DOES NOT FADE OVER TIME.

LET'S REJOICE IN THE RETURN OF KAZALIM THE CURSE LORD, WHY DON'T WE?

NOW, NOW.

THAT ALL HAPPENED TWO CENTURIES AGO, RIGHT?

...THAT I HAPPENED ACROSS THE BOSS.

...IT WAS INDEED A STROKE OF LUCK...

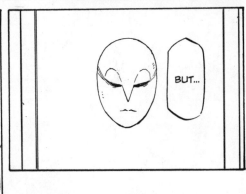

BUT...

TEN YEARS AGO, MY SOUL WAS TRULY ON THE VERGE OF EVAPORATING INTO NOTHING.

IT HAD WITHERED AWAY FROM THE LACK OF A BODY.

IF I HADN'T POSSESSED THE BOSS, I WOULD INDEED BE DEAD.

"BOSS"...

A SPECIAL ORDER FROM THE SORCEROUS DYNASTY OF THALION?

YES, I KNOW.

CLINK

IT COST *QUITE* A FAIR AMOUNT TO ACQUIRE.

I'D APPRECIATE IT IF YOU DIDN'T COMPLAIN ABOUT THE ABILITIES OF YOUR NEW BODY.

...BUT IT'S STILL FAR PREFERABLE TO NOT HAVING A MATERIAL BODY OF MY OWN AT ALL.

IT'S FRAGILE, AND ITS APPEARANCE IS NOT TO MY LIKING...

PUFF

Bfft

...VERY WELL.

S-SORRY! IT'S JUST, YOUR BODY DOESN'T MATCH YOUR VIBE AT ALL!

ARE YOU GOING TO GET OVER IT OR NOT, LAPLACE?

GA HYA HYA HYA HYA HYA HYA!!

SHUT THE HELL UP ALREADY!!

BWA HA HA HA HA!

SINCE I MUST PLAY THE ROLE OF SECRETARY UNTIL MY STRENGTH IS FULLY RETURNED...

...I SHALL MAKE EFFORTS TO ACT THE PART.

HEY, DO YOU MIND IF WE GET DOWN TO BUSINESS?

...ABOUT THE WESTERN HOLY CHURCH, DIDN'T YOU?

YOU FIGURED SOMETHING OUT...

I'LL TELL YA STRAIGHT OUT. NO MIND GAMES.

IF THE PRESIDENT CALLS YA BOSS, THEN YER *MY* BOSS, TOO.

YEP.

THEY WOULDN'T LEAVE ANYTHIN' REAL BAD OUT WHERE ANYONE CAN SEE IT.

OF COURSE, THEY LET WORSHIP-PERS GO THERE FOR SERVICES.

I DIDN'T SEE ANYTHIN' FISHY IN THEIR HEAD-QUARTERS.

I THOUGHT, MAYBE THERE'D BE SOMETHIN' IN THE INNER CLOISTER, WHERE ONLY THE HOLY EMPEROR CAN GO.

AND THEN...

I'll just take a peek at the peak.

SO I DECIDED TO HEAD UP THEIR SACRED MOUNTAIN.

WHAT THE?

AND I GOT BLASTED TO PIECES!

...THIS BIG HOITY-TOITY VAMPIRE GUY STEPS OUT...

...AND STARTS SHOOTIN' RED BEAMS OF LIGHT...

YOU COULDN'T KILL HIM EVEN IF YOU TRIED.

UH, HOW *ARE* YOU ALIVE?

THAT WAS A BAD ONE. THOUGHT I WAS DEAD FOR SURE.

...SO WHAT'S A VAMPIRE DOIN' THERE?

THAT WAS S'POSED TO BE A HOLY PLACE...

THE QUESTION IS HIS IDENTITY.

...AND A VAMPIRE, AT THAT— A HIGHER SPECIES.

SO A POWERFUL MEMBER OF THE LUMINIST CHURCH IS A MAJIN...

AND HE WAS DRESSED IN SOME KINDA CHURCH VESTMENTS.

MEANIN' HE WAS AFFILIATED WITH THE CHURCH.

DO YOU KNOW SOMETHING ABOUT THIS, KAZALIM?

PERHAPS MORE THAN JUST A MAJIN.

YOU KNOW WHAT IT IS?!

...WHICH EMITS BLOOD IN THE FORM OF MAGI-CULES.

THAT IS A TECHNIQUE CALLED "BLOOD RAY"...

YOU SAID HE EMITTED A RED BEAM.

YEP.

DEMON LORD VALENTINE.

ALSO KNOWN AS THE "BLOODY LORD."

THAT WAS HIS SIGNATURE TECHNIQUE.

DEMON LORD?! YOU FOR REAL?

YOU MADE THE RIGHT CHOICE TO FLEE, LAPLACE.

HE WAS MY EQUAL WHEN I WAS AT THE HEIGHT OF MY STRENGTH.

Whoaaa...

I HAD MANY BATTLES WITH HIM, BACK IN THE DAY.

IT LED TO THE DESTRUCTION OF MANY VILLAGES AND SETTLEMENTS CAUGHT BETWEEN US.

THAT WAS HOW WE STARTED THE CUSTOM OF TALKING THINGS OUT AND SOLVING DISPUTES WITH A VOTE.

AND THAT WAS THE WALPURGIS COUNCIL?

YES.

REQUIRING THREE VOTES FOR A MOTION WAS A HOLDOVER FROM WHEN THERE WERE ONLY SEVEN DEMON LORDS.

... SHUT UP, YOU MAGGOT.

PRESIDENT, I STILL CAN'T GET USED TO YOU LOOKING LIKE THAT!

...WHAT WAS HE DOING IN A PLACE LIKE THAT?

SO, ASSUMING THAT REALLY *WAS* DEMON LORD VALENTINE...

...IS THAT THE HOLY EMPEROR IS A DEMON LORD...

...I SUPPOSE.

THE MOST LIKELY ANSWER...

THE VALENTINE I KNEW SAW HUMANS AND DEMI-HUMANS AS NOTHING BUT FOOD.

IF HE IS NOW STYLING HIMSELF AS THE PROTECTOR OF HUMANITY...

...THEN HE'S UP TO SOMETHING.

HMM, ALL RIGHT... BUT HOW'S HE FOOLIN' HINATA, THEN?

IF SHE KNEW THE HOLY EMPEROR WAS A DEMON LORD...

...SHE'D NEVER STAY QUIET ABOUT IT. I MEAN, SHE *HATES* MONSTERS.

IN ANY CASE, THIS IS INFORMATION WE CAN USE.

WELL DONE, LAPLACE.

WHICH IS WHY HE MUST BE UP TO *SOMETHING.*

AH, THAT.

HE SAID HE WAS GONNA FORCE FALMUTH TO DO SOMETHIN', RIGHT?

DID CLAYMAN MANAGE TO TRIGGER HIS AWAKENING?

THAT'S THE END OF MY REPORT.

I KNEW IT WOULD DRIVE THAT GREEDY KING TO ACTION.

...SO I LEAKED WORD OF TEMPEST'S SPECIAL PRODUCTS.

I WAS LOOKING TO PARE DOWN THAT SOURCE OF STRENGTH...

YOU KNOW HOW THAT COUNTRY HAS A BUNCH OF OTHER-WORLDERS?

AND
...?

I ONLY WANTED TO SOFTEN FALMUTH UP A BIT...

...BUT THEY GOT TURNED INTO PULP.

WIPED OUT. BY A SINGLE SLIME.

THEY ROLLED IN WITH AN INVASION FORCE OF TWENTY THOUSAND.

OH, NO, THEY WERE QUITE SERIOUS.

WAS FALMUTH NOT EVEN TRYING TO FIGHT TEMPEST?!

W-WHAT?!

DEFEATING TWENTY THOUSAND ON HIS OWN IS ONE THING...

I WONDER WHAT IT IS ABOUT THAT SLIME.

...BUT TO SURVIVE A BATTLE AGAINST HINATA— NOW THAT'S THE REAL SURPRISE.

WE WERE BEATEN TO THE PUNCH.

NO.

NOT A SINGLE SOUL WAS LEFT BEHIND.

S-SO DID YOU GET A BUNCH OF HUMAN SOULS, AT LEAST?

SIGH...

MEANING...

...THE ATTEMPT TO CLAIM THE SOULS FOR CLAYMAN'S AWAKENING FAILED.

AND BECAUSE EURAZANIA HAD EVACUATED IN ADVANCE OF MILIM'S RAMPAGE...

...THERE WERE NO SOULS TO BE HARVESTED THERE, EITHER.

Oh, dear.

HOW-EVER...

Don't play with my food.

I'll go cheer him up later.

...BUT SO HAS HE, SOUNDS LIKE.

I'VE HAD A ROUGH GO OF IT...

A SINGLE MAJIN WIPED OUT AN ARMY OF THOUSANDS.

PLOP
ポ

PLOP
ポ

WHADDA YA MEAN?

IT'S TO OUR BENEFIT THAT FALMUTH LOST, I THINK.

THE WESTERN HOLY CHURCH, WITH ITS LOFTY IDEALS...

...CAN'T OVERLOOK SUCH AN EVENT, CAN THEY?

AND IF THEY'RE GOING TO DEAL WITH SUCH A DANGEROUS MAJIN...

...THEN HINATA HERSELF MUST BE INVOLVED.

SHUNK

EXACTLY. IT SUITS OUR PURPOSES.

SO THE PRESENCE OF A LAND OF MONSTERS THAT DRAWS THE CHURCH'S EYE...

AND THE BIGGEST OBSTACLE TO CONTROLLING THE WESTERN NATIONS IS LUMINISM.

I GETCHA.

CRUNCH

MUNCH MUNCH

MUNCH MUNCH

OH?

THE BIGGEST WRENCH IN THE WORKS WAS YOUR REPORT, LAPLACE.

...BUT THE THRUST OF OUR PLAN IS STILL INTACT.

WHAT HAPPENED WAS NOT SOMETHING I ANTICIPATED...

WELL... IF YA JUST WANT TO LURE OUT A DEMON LORD, WE GOT OPTIONS.

...BUT KNOWING DEMON LORD VALENTINE IS THERE MAKES THAT MUCH HARDER.

I'D LIKE TO INVESTIGATE THE WESTERN HOLY CHURCH MORE...

I WAS GOING TO ASK YOU TO INFILTRATE IT AGAIN.

HE MAKES IT SOUND LIKE IT'S MY FAULT... No fair...

YOU CAN DO A LOT WITH AN ALLIANCE OF THREE DEMON LORDS, CAN'T YA?

CLAYMAN, MILIM, FREY.

SO USE THEM, AND CALL UP...

...THE WALPURGIS COUNCIL.

SQUISHY SLIME.

...WHAT'S YOUR NEXT MOVE?

NOW...

RIGHT?

BY YOUR STANDARDS, IT'S BRILLIANT.

CLANK
ジャラ

WHERE
....?

WHAT
HAPPENED
...

AH!

DO YOU HAVE ANY IDEA WHO I AM?!

W—WHERE AM I?! WHO ARE YOU?!

ARE YOU AWAKE?

I AM THE RULER OF THE GREAT NATION OF FALMUTH!

KING ED- MARIS !!

I KNOW.

I AM CHARGED WITH INTER- ROGATING PRISON- ERS.

I AM SHION, FIRST SECRETARY OF CHAN- CELLOR RIMURU.

YOU ARE IN AN UNDER- GROUND CELL IN THE JURA TEMPEST FEDERATION.

I-INTERROGATING...

...P-PRISONERS?

YOU WILL TELL US EVERYTHING YOU KNOW ABOUT THE STATE OF AFFAIRS IN FALMUTH.

I HAVE BEEN GIVEN PERMISSION TO DO ANYTHING TO MAKE YOU TALK...

...SHORT OF ENDING YOUR LIFE.

BUT...

...SPEAKING PERSONALLY...

I BELIEVE LORD RIMURU WAS GIVING ME A CHANCE FOR VENGEANCE.

Life again...?

AND DESPITE THAT, I WAS GIVEN THE GIFT OF LIFE AGAIN.

I LOST BECAUSE I WAS TOO WEAK TO SURVIVE.

...I DO NOT BEAR MUCH ANGER AT HAVING BEEN KILLED.

I AM NOT OPPOSED TO COOPERATING WITH YOU—

HOWEVER, SOME THINGS CANNOT BE FORGIVEN.

HE WOULD NOT LOOK KINDLY UPON THE MONSTERS UNDER HIS EMPLOY HARMING HUMANS WITHOUT GOOD REASON.

BY THE WAY, ARE YOU AWARE...

...THAT LORD RIMURU LOVES HUMANS?

YOUR DECISIONS...

...FORCED LORD RIMURU TO KILL HUMANS.

IN THAT CASE, I WILL SPEAK FREELY WITH YOU.

I... I SEE.

ONE THOUSAND WOUNDS WOULD NOT BE ENOUGH.

I WILL ENSURE THAT YOU FOREVER RUE...

...THE FACT THAT YOU WERE GIVEN LIFE IN THE FIRST PLACE.

YOU HAVE STAINED HIS PRISTINE HANDS...

...WITH HUMAN BLOOD!!

EYAAAH!!

UNLESS YOU WANT TO KEEP YOUR KING'S SECRETS...

IF YOU HAVE ANYTHING TO TELL US ABOUT THE CHURCH, I WOULD SUGGEST YOU DO IT NOW.

...AND TURN OUT LIKE THAT SORCEROR RAZEN OVER THERE.

TWIK

PWOK

AAAAH

JOLT

AAH...

TEK
コッ

TEK
コッ

THEY'RE NOT FROM THAT DEMON WOMAN!

H... HELP ME...

THOSE FOOT-STEPS...

TEK
コッ

TEK
コッ

I MADE A MISTAKE. I WISH TO EXPLAIN MYSELF TO YOUR LORD.

YOU THERE... GIRL? LET ME OUT OF HERE...

I KNOW WHO YOU ARE.

I AM THE KING OF FAL-MUTH—

PLEASE... GRANT ME AN AUDIENCE...

HAVE YOU ALREADY FORGOTTEN MY VOICE?

...!!

HELP...

H-HEL...

EEP!

THE PEOPLE OF FALMUTH ARE GOING TO SUFFER TERRIBLY IN THE DAYS AHEAD.

IF YOU WANT TO PLEAD YOUR CASE, I SHOULDN'T BE FIRST ON YOUR LIST.

SPEND YOUR TIME THINKING UNTIL THEN.

WE WILL DECIDE WHAT TO DO WITH OUR PRISONERS AT THE MEETING.

THIS IS THE KARMA THAT YOU AND I BEAR.

THAT'S MILIM'S TERRITORY ...

PUPPET NATION DISTAVE

FORGOTTEN CITY OF DRAGONS

CLAYMAN'S SENDING AN ARMY?

YES.

BASED ON THEIR PATH, IT SEEMS THEY'RE HEADING FOR THE FORGOTTEN CITY OF DRAGONS.

THEY NUMBER ABOUT THIRTY THOUSAND.

WHOA.

HOLD ON A SEC.

SOMEONE'S COMING.

THD THD THD

BRR-HRR

SOME-
ONE I
KNOW.

Let's
go.

IN
TIME?
FOR
WHAT?

I'M
GLAD
WE
MADE
IT IN
TIME.

IT'S
GOOD TO
SEE YOU
AGAIN,
RIMURU.

UH... WHAT'S UP, FUZE?

IT'S NOT MUCH, BUT WE BROUGHT THE MOST MOBILE ONES WITH US.

IT'LL BE A LITTLE WHILE BEFORE THE MAIN FORCE ARRIVES.

HEH.

WHAT BRINGS YOU HERE TODAY?

ALLOW US TO TAKE PART IN THE FIGHT AGAINST FALMUTH.

WE'VE COME HERE TO UPHOLD THE SECURITY TREATY BETWEEN BLUMUND AND TEMPEST.

...WHAT?

CHAPTER 74 Monster-and-Man Summit I

HUH ?

IT'S OVER ?

...BUT IT WOULD SEEM THEY MISSED ONE ANOTHER ALONG THE ROAD.

WE SENT AN ENVOY WITH THE MESSAGE...

FROM WHAT MJÖLLMILE TOLD US, IT'S ONLY BEEN TWO WEEKS SINCE FALMUTH DECLARED WAR!!

WHAT DOES THAT MEAN ?!

NOTICE: THIRTY HORSE-BACK UNITS APPROACH-ING.

UM... LISTEN, FUZE...

THEY ARE LED BY GAZEL DWARGO.

IT'S JUST ONE AFTER THE OTHER.

VERY WELL.

JUST WARN ME ABOUT THE DANGEROUS ONES.

IT'S KIND OF ANNOYING TO GET A REPORT FOR EVERY ONE OF THEM.

THE ADVANCED VERSION OF "MAGIC SENSE" IS "UNIVERSAL DETECT," WHICH VASTLY INCREASES RANGE AND PRECISION.

I UNDERSTAND YOU ARE A DEMON LORD NOW.

THINGS HAVE... HAPPENED.

IT IS GOOD TO SEE YOU AGAIN, RIMURU.

THU-
THUD

I WOULD LIKE TO JOIN YOU, THEN.

I WAS GOING TO HAVE A MEETING WITH MY PRINCIPAL OFFICERS ABOUT OUR FUTURE PLANS.

TWITCH

DEMON LORD...?

I'M TELLING YOU, I'VE HAD A TIME.

I HAD A FEELING YOU'D MAKE A NAME FOR YOURSELF... BUT A DEMON LORD?

YOU EXPECT ME TO JUST IGNORE THAT?!

WHAT DOES THIS MEAN?!

DEMON LORD...?

I'M NOT ASKING WHERE THE BATHROOM IS!!

YOU NEED TO PEE? GO BACK AND TAKE A LEFT—

...ABOUT THE WAR WITH FALMUTH ALREADY BEING OVER?

DOES IT HAVE ANYTHING TO DO WITH WHAT YOU WERE SAYING...

WHAT DO YOU MEAN, YOU'RE A DEMON LORD?

I WOULD LIKE A SERIOUS ANSWER, RIMURU.

THE FALMUTH ARMY WAS THE SACRIFICE—

I BECAME A DEMON LORD BECAUSE I HAD TO.

KING GAZEL IS CORRECT.

WAIT, RIMURU.

ZSH

FLAP FLAP

WHEN THE FALMUTH ROYAL ARMY WAS ON THE MOVE...

...WHY DID THEY SIMPLY *VANISH?*

IF YOU KNOW, THEN I WOULD APPRECIATE AN ANSWER.

I HEARD THAT IN VESTA'S REPORT, TOO.

THAT'S WHAT I'M TELLING YOU, I—

HUH? UM, HANG ON...

HE SAID, "ON THE MARCH, THE FALMUTH ROYAL ARMY SUDDENLY WAS NO LONGER DETECTABLE."

"WE ARE INVESTIGATING THE CAUSE."

OH. I SEE WHAT THEY'RE DOING.

!

VESTA SAID THAT?

...IS EVEN MORE FRIGHTENING THAN NUCLEAR WEAPONS, WHICH AT LEAST HAVE LAYERS OF PROCEDURE TO THEM.

BUT AN INDIVIDUAL CAPABLE OF WIPING OUT AN ARMY OF THOUSANDS ON A WHIM...

VESTA WOULD HAVE GIVEN THEM AN ACCURATE REPORT OF WHAT HAPPENED.

THEY'RE TRYING TO CAST DOUBT ON THE FACT THAT I MASSACRED AN ARMY OF TWENTY THOUSAND.

AS YOU HEARD, THE FALMUTH ARMY HAS GONE MISSING.

IT'S TRUE THAT ANNOUNCING THE TRUTH WOULD ONLY LEAD TO CONFUSION AND CHAOS.

"COVER-UP" IS SUCH A DIRTY WORD. AND YET...

UH... SO, FUZE...

SIGH...

...

NO, I DIDN'T EXPECT HIM TO BELIEVE IT.

AFTER ALL, I ALREADY SAID THEY WERE A SACRIFICE.

GOT IT. MESSAGE RECEIVED.

THE FALMUTH ARMY IS MISSING.

MAYBE I'M JUST TIRED FROM RIDING SO HARD. MUST'VE BEEN HEARING THINGS.

OF COURSE.

...BUT I WON'T BE A SPECTATOR.

I DO TRUST YOU...

BUT I INSIST ON ATTENDING THE STRATEGY MEETING, TOO.

I'M VERY GOOD AT MANIPULATING MEMORIES.

GRIN

YIKES!

SIIIGH...

IF YOU ARE WORRIED, ALLOW ME TO HANDLE IT.

WHAT?

FUZE IS FINE.

YOU TRUST THAT MAN, RIMURU.

I DO.

BUT IF ANY OF HIS SUB-ORDINATES HEAR ABOUT THIS, DO IT ON THEM.

WE WON'T WANT IT GETTING AROUND, EVEN IF THEY MEAN WELL.

VERY GOOD, MASTER.

HOW DO I REPORT THIS TO THE KING?

BECAUSE I KNOW THAT HE TRUSTS US.

I'll show you the way.

Sorry, where's the bathroom?

BUT HE CAME RIGHT TO OUR AID.

IF HE BELIEVED FALMUTH'S STORY, HE COULD HAVE ANY NUMBER OF EXCUSES TO IGNORE OUR AGREEMENT.

!

HMPH. THEN *THEY'LL* BE THE REAL PROBLEM.

IF IT ISN'T THE EMPEROR WHO PREFERS TO DWELL UNDER THE SOIL.

MY, MY, MY.

ズシ

135

WHAT A SURPRISE.

I WOULD NOT EXPECT A COWARD LIKE YOU TO AID A DEMON LORD.

FSH...

HEY, DON'T SULK!

REPORT...

NO HOSTILITY WAS DETECTED, SO I DID NOT INFORM YOU.

WHO IS THIS GUY...?

HE DIDN'T SET OFF MY "UNIVERSAL DETECT" SKILL?!

WHAT, SOKA?

LORD RIMURU.

BUT IF HE'S NOT AN ENEMY, WHY IS HE HERE?

A NOBLE FROM THALION?!

THE HEAD OF A NOBLE FAMILY, APPARENTLY...

HE IS AN ENVOY FROM THE SORCEROUS DYNASTY OF THALION.

It seems so.

Did she call that one "Rimuru"?

WHY IS SUCH A PRESTIGIOUS FIGURE HERE IN PERSON?!

AND HE'S EREN'S—

GLARE

RIMURU...

I SEE. SO YOU...

YOU ARE THE ACCURSED DEMON LORD RIMURU WHO BAMBOOZLED MY DAUGHTER?!

BOOM

REPORT: THIS IS A SYNTHESIZED SPELL OF FLAME AND EXPLOSIVE MAGIC.

IT INVOLVES A HIGHLY ADVANCED SEQUENCE IN WHICH THE CASTER MUST EXERCISE CONTROL OVER HIS OWN MAGIC.

I DON'T CARE HOW IT WORKS!

WH... WHAT ?!

WE NEED TO STOP—

OH.

SMACK

Da...

HEY !!

WHAT ARE YOU DOING HERE, DAD ?!

EREN ?!

MY DEEPEST APOLO-GIES.

"DAD"?!

I WAS IN A PANIC, BECAUSE THE REPORT SAID MY DAUGHTER HAD BEEN ABDUCTED BY A DEMON LORD.

THAT MAGIC SPELL, HOWEVER...

Of course you'd jump to conclusions, Dad!

No, my lord, I gave an accurate report.

HE'S AS OVER-PROTEC-TIVE AS I REMEMBER.

YOU *KNOW* THAT GUY?!

UH, PLEASE DO.

RIMURU, CAN I INTRODUCE MY FATHER TO YOU?

I'M RIMURU TEMPEST.

NICE TO MEET YOU, TOO.

...CHANCELLOR OF THE GREAT FOREST OF JURA AND LEADER OF MONSTERS.

A PLEASURE TO MEET YOU...

...ERALD GRIMWALD.

HE IS AN ARCHDUKE OF THE SORCEROUS DYNASTY OF THALION...

OF COURSE...

...THAT IS NOT THE *ONLY* THING.

SO... ARE YOU ONLY HERE ABOUT EREN?

...WHAT MY DAUGHTER SEES IN YOU.

I WANTED TO UNDERSTAND...

...FOR THE PURPOSE OF DECIDING FURTHER RELATIONS WITH YOUR COUNTRY.

I WANTED TO ASSESS YOUR CHARACTER WITH MY OWN EYES...

...THAT YOU ARE NOT SOMEONE WHO FALLS FOR EMPTY BLUFFS.

BUT I DO KNOW...

I CAN'T SAY YET.

AND WHAT DO YOU THINK?

FORGIVE ME FOR TESTING YOU.

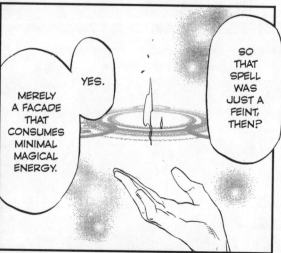

MERELY A FACADE THAT CONSUMES MINIMAL MAGICAL ENERGY.

YES.

SO THAT SPELL WAS JUST A FEINT, THEN?

IT'S HARD TO TELL IF HE'S SHREWD, OR JUST AN ECCENTRIC FOOL.

DON'T YOU DARE LAY A FINGER ON HER, GAZEL!!

IS THAT YOU, ERYUNE?

I HARDLY RECOGNIZE YOU.

IT'S GOOD TO SEE YOU AGAIN, KING GAZEL.

Eren's brutal...

I DON'T HAVE ENOUGH INFORMATION TO JUDGE HIM YET.

...BUT WOULD IT BE POSSIBLE FOR ME TO ATTEND THIS MEETING YOU WERE SPEAKING ABOUT?

I REALIZE I MAY BE SPEAKING OUT OF TURN HERE...

AH, YES.

PSST コソ

LORD RIMURU.

WE MIGHT NOT BE ABLE TO FIT INTO THE USUAL MEETING HALL.

VERY WELL. YOU WILL HAVE A SEAT THERE.

BUT THESE UNEXPECTED VISITORS ARE SWELLING OUR RANKS.

I THANK YOU.

HEY, RIMURU.

I WILL ARRANGE FOR A LARGER SPACE, BUT FOR NOW...

SO *YOU* WERE THE CAUSE OF THE STORM DRAGON'S DISAPPEAR-ANCE TWO YEARS AGO.

I GUESS YOU COULD SAY THAT.

HMM. I SEE...

...AND NOW WE MUST CONTEND WITH THE STORM DRAGON?

WE WILL BE BUSY ENOUGH WITH THE ARRIVAL OF A NEW DEMON LORD...

I can do water blades!

...THE WORLD OUTSIDE WAS SENT INTO A PANIC, I GUESS!?

SO WHILE I WAS BUSY IN THE CAVE GAINING ALL THOSE SKILLS...

THEY ARE SURE TO NOTICE HIS RETURN IMMEDIATELY.

...

INDEED.

THEY ARE ESPECIALLY HOSTILE TO THE DRAGON, AFTER ALL.

THE WESTERN HOLY CHURCH WILL NOT SIT IDLY BY.

146

SAY, KING GAZEL...

BUT THAT WASN'T MADE WITH THE EXPECTATION OF A THREAT ON THE SCALE OF THE WESTERN HOLY CHURCH.

THERE IS A PACT OF MUTUAL COOPERATION BETWEEN TEMPEST AND DWARGON IN THE CASE OF NATIONAL PERIL.

YOU WOULD ASK THAT OF ME, RIMURU?

IF WE GET INTO A FIGHT WITH THE WESTERN HOLY CHURCH, WHOSE SIDE WILL YOU TAKE?

IF A SENIOR PUPIL THINKS SO, THAT'S GOOD TO HEAR.

I SEE.

WE HAVE NO REASON *NOT* TO SUPPORT TEMPEST, WHO IS AN ACTUAL FRIEND.

DWARGON HAS NO OBLIGATION TOWARD THE WESTERN HOLY CHURCH.

STILL, YOU DON'T KNOW HOW OTHER COUNTRIES WILL REACT.

IT'S A GOOD THING THIS CONVERSATION IS DISCREET...

YOU OUGHT TO LEARN A BIT MORE STATE-CRAFT.

Plus, for Lord Veldora, we want...

That's the last chair we need.

How many more chairs?

FOR A SO-CALLED "WAR," THE OUTCOME SEEMS EXTREMELY ONE-SIDED.

AH... YES, SIR.

...THE DEMON LORD WHO CAUSED TWENTY THOUSAND DEATHS WILL ALWAYS APPEAR THE GREATER EVIL.

TO THE REST OF THE WORLD, WHICH IS NOT AWARE OF HOW THIS CAME TO HAPPEN...

AND IF THE WESTERN HOLY CHURCH DECLARES YOU AN "ENEMY OF GOD"...

YOU SHOULD ASSUME THE WESTERN NATIONS WILL BE HOSTILE.

AND THAT MIGHT PUT A LOT OF PRESSURE ON COUNTRIES WE'RE FRIENDLY WITH.

I DON'T WANT THAT.

AT THIS POINT, I CANNOT SAY.

WHAT DOES THE SORCEROUS DYNASTY OF THALION THINK?

WAS IT EREN...

...WHO URGED YOU TO BECOME A DEMON LORD?

BUT...

IF WORD OF THE DEATH TOLL SPREADS AMONG THE WESTERN NATIONS, THAT WILL PLACE MY COUNTRY IN A DIFFICULT SITUATION.

IF SO, THEN WE CANNOT BE PASSIVE OBSERVERS IN THIS.

NO...

ZMF

WHAT DO YOU MEAN, GAZEL?

REST ASSURED, THAT WILL NOT BE A PROBLEM.

THE TRUTH WILL NOT SPREAD FURTHER.

THE BODIES HAVE VANISHED. THERE ARE NO SURVIVORS, ASIDE FROM PRISONERS.

IS THAT CORRECT, RIMURU?

YES, THAT'S RIGHT.

IF IT MEANS I MUST BEAR FURTHER SIN, MY RESOLVE WILL NOT BE SHAKEN.

WHEN I MADE UP MY MIND TO RESURRECT ALL THOSE PEOPLE, I WAS READY.

WELL? WHAT'S THE STORY YOU'RE GOING TO TELL?

AS YOU SHOULD.

A KING MUST NOT DWELL ON REGRETS.

YOU SEEM TO BE PREPARED FOR ANY OUTCOME IN THIS MATTER.

NOW THAT WE HAVE ALL BECOME ACQUAINTED WITH EACH OTHER...

...I WOULD LIKE TO BRIEFLY NAME THE REPRESENTATIVES OF EACH NATION PRESENT.

FROM THE ARMORED NATION OF DWARGON...

...KING GAZEL DWARGO.

FROM THE ANIMAL KINGDOM OF EURAZANIA...

...ALBIS, LEADER OF THE THREE BEASTKETEERS.

I just had to volunteer...

WHY AM I IN SUCH A MAJOR POSITION?

...MR. FUZE.

FROM BLUMUND, THE GUILD-MASTER AND ASSISTANT DIRECTOR OF INTELLI-GENCE...

...ARCHDUKE ERALD GRIMWALD.

FROM THE SORCEROUS DYNASTY OF THALION...

...RIMURU TEMPEST.

...CHAN-CELLOR AND DEMON LORD...

LASTLY, FROM THE JURA TEMPEST FEDERA-TION...

UH—HUH...

JUST DON'T MESS THINGS UP, OKAY?

HEY—

...BUT I GAVE HIM MANGA TO READ, BECAUSE IF HE SPEAKS IT'LL CAUSE CHAOS.

I HAVE VELDORA HERE, TOO, AS A SPECIAL ADVISOR...

HE'S ALREADY LOST IN IT.

AND SOME OF THESE PEOPLE ARE UNKNOWN VARIABLES.

SHALL WE BEGIN?

I HEARD THAT YOU WERE FROM SHIZU'S HOME...

SEVERAL ATTENDEES ARE CURIOUS ABOUT MY ROOTS AND MY CONNECTION TO VELDORA.

FIRST, I'LL EXPLAIN THE SITUATION.

SO I TOLD THEM, IN SHORT, THAT I WAS A HUMAN FROM ANOTHER WORLD...

...THAT I WAS REBORN AS A SLIME...

...THAT I WAS ATTACKED BY HINATA WHEN RETURNING FROM ABROAD...

...AND THAT I ONLY ARRIVED HOME AFTER THE INVASION.

AND THAT IS HOW...

...THE FALMUTH ARMY BECAME MY SACRIFICE.

I CONCLUDED WITH MY BECOMING A DEMON LORD.

AS A RESULT, I AWOKE AS A DEMON LORD.

NOW...

...WHAT I'VE JUST TOLD YOU IS THE TRUTH.

BUT THE STORY WE MAKE PUBLIC WILL BE VERY DIFFERENT.

DIFFERENT HOW? AND WHY?

MURMUR MURMUR

...THEN FEAR WILL DASH HIS PLANS.

IF RIMURU'S HOPE IS FOR MAN AND MONSTER TO LIVE IN HARMONY...

WHEN ONE REACHES OUT HIS HAND IN FRIENDSHIP, BUT IT IS COVERED IN BLOOD, NO ONE WOULD TAKE THAT HAND.

HOW- EVER...

THE SAME WILL BE TRUE IF WE ASSIGN BLAME TO HIS FOLLOWERS.

HIS VERY EXISTENCE IS A LEGEND, AND HIS ACTIONS BRING ONLY MISERY.

...IF THE *STORM DRAGON* DID IT, THAT IS ANOTHER MATTER.

THEY WILL HAVE NO CHOICE BUT TO BELIEVE IT.

WOULD YOU SHUT UP BACK THERE, OLD MAN?

A GENIUS, EH?

Heh...

THAT WOULD BE A MUCH BETTER NARRATIVE.

DAD...

I'D RATHER SAY THAT THE BIRTH OF THE DEMON LORD MADE IT POSSIBLE TO OPEN UP INTERACTIONS WITH THE STORM DRAGON...

I DON'T WANT TO BE HATED BECAUSE MY DAUGHTER CAUSED THE BIRTH OF A NEW DEMON LORD.

I SUPPORT THIS SCENARIO AS WELL.

POOR GUY... HE'S JUST DOING WHAT'S BEST FOR HIS DAUGHTER.

!!

SHUNK

BUT IT'S SO SNEAKY.

THERE IS NO PROBLEM AT ALL.

ESPECIALLY BECAUSE VELDORA WILL BE BEARING THE BLAME FOR MY ACTS...

IF THERE ANY OBJECTIONS, I WANT TO HEAR THEM.

I HAVE DECIDED THAT I WILL SHARE YOUR KARMA.

USE THE REPUTATION OF THE STORM DRAGON ALL YOU LIKE.

BY THE WAY, RIMURU, WHAT WILL YOU DO WITH THE PRISONERS?

THERE'S NO TELLING WHAT STORIES THEY MIGHT SPREAD.

AH, YES...

COOL... THANKS.

HE REALLY IS FRIENDS WITH THE DRAGON...

I'LL NEED TO DESTROY THE KINGDOM OF FALMUTH.

THIS IS QUITE A DIRECT STATEMENT.

WILL YOU WAGE WAR ON THEM?

FIRST, I WILL RELEASE THEIR KING AND FORCE HIM TO PAY REPARATIONS TO OUR COUNTRY.

YOU MIGHT CALL IT THAT.

BUT I WON'T USE AN ARMY.

THAT'S MY HOPE.

I CAN'T IMAGINE THEY'LL ACTUALLY PAY REPARATIONS...

I HATE TO SAY THIS, BUT ASIDE FROM A SMALL GROUP, THEIR NOBLES ARE ROTTEN TO THE CORE.

CIVIL WAR...?

MY ACTUAL GOAL IS TO CAUSE A CIVIL WAR WITHIN FALMUTH.

THE REPARATIONS ARE ONLY A MEANS TO AN END.

...

I'LL MAKE IT COLLAPSE...

...SO THAT A NEW COUNTRY CAN ARISE FROM THE ASHES.

A COUNTRY WITH THE CHAMPION YOUM AS ITS NEW KING.

YOU'RE NOT SUR- PRISED BY THIS, YOUNG MAN.

THAT'S RIGHT, YOUR MAJESTY... HE ALREADY TOLD ME ABOUT THIS PLAN.

THANK- FULLY, HE IS BE- LOVED BY THE PEO- PLE THERE.

HMM... WELL, YOUR SPIRIT IS FIRM.

BUT ARE YOU READY FOR THIS?

GRIT...

OHHHH

THIS ROLE WAS PLACED ON MY SHOULDERS OUT OF TRUST.

THUMP

I'M GOING TO GIVE IT EVERYTHING I'VE GOT.

BA HA HA!

idiot...

AFTER ALL, WHAT MAN DOESN'T WANT TO LOOK GOOD BEFORE THE WOMAN HE LOVES?

...HE IS A PROPER HEROIC KING, JUST LIKE YOU.

I, GRUCIUS, WILL KEEP MY EYE ON HIM UNTIL THE DAY...

KING OF THE DWARVES, YOU HAVE MY GUARANTEE.

HE MAY BE STUPID, BUT HE IS NOT IRRESPON-SIBLE.

K-TUNK

HEH.

IS THAT SO?

NOW...

IF ANYONE HAS ANY OTHER THOUGHTS ABOUT THIS PLAN, I'D LIKE TO HEAR THEM.

VERY GOOD, THEN. ASK ME IF YOU SHOULD NEED HELP.

GOOD TO KNOW.

IT'S POSSIBLE THAT BLUMUND MIGHT BE ABLE TO ASSIST YOU WITH THIS.

FUZE, GO AHEAD.

MAY I?

REALLY ?!

IF ALL GOES WELL, HE MIGHT ARRANGE THINGS FOR US.

I BELIEVE WE MIGHT BE ABLE TO NEGOTIATE WITH HIM.

IN FALMUTH THERE IS A NOBLEMAN NAMED MARQUIS MULLER WHO IS A DISTANT RELATIVE OF THE KING OF BLUMUND.

MIGHTY FIGURES SPEAKING HONESTLY ACROSS NATIONAL LINES!

HOW DELIGHT-FUL THIS IS!

FWA HA HA HA! FASCI-NATING.

LET ME ASK YOU SOME-THING, FUZE.

!

IT MAKES ME FEEL FOOLISH FOR BEING WARY.

THUNK

YOU ARE HERE AS A REPRESEN-TATIVE OF BLUMUND, AREN'T YOU?

WHAT? ME?

Thanks.

WHAT DO YOU MEAN ...?

WHY DID YOUR COUNTRY FORM DIPLOMATIC TIES WITH TEMPEST?

I WANT TO KNOW WHAT THE KING OF BLUMUND IS THINKING.

IT DOESN'T SEEM LIKE HAVING AN OFFICIAL RELATIONSHIP WAS NECESSARY TO ME.

...AND WAITED TO SEE HOW THE WESTERN HOLY CHURCH REACTS?

COULDN'T YOU HAVE STUCK TO PROFITABLE TRADING...

IF YOU'LL FORGIVE ME FOR SAYING, YOURS IS NOT A MAJOR COUNTRY.

YES, I KNOW THAT...

SCRUB

SCRUB

WE MUST HAVE MUTUAL TRUST AND COEXISTENCE.

BUT...

IT IS THE ONLY WAY.

YOU'RE CORRECT, ARCHDUKE ERALD.

I HAD THAT SAME THOUGHT, AS DID VERYARD, ANOTHER NOBLE OF MY COUNTRY.

IF WE DO NOT MAINTAIN TIES, IT WILL BE THE END OF US!

THAT COUNTRY DEFEATED THE ORC LORD AND CHARYBDIS, DID IT NOT?

B-BUT...

I HAD A FEELING THERE WAS MORE TO THAT KING THAN MET THE EYE.

THAT WAS WHAT THE KING SAID BEFORE RIMURU CAME TO VISIT BLUMUND.

...BETTER TO SIDE WITH THE MASTER OF MONSTERS THAN THE WESTERN HOLY CHURCH.

IF WE ARE GOING TO THROW OURSELVES TO THE WHIMS OF FATE...

LUMINISM HAS FEW CONVERTS WITHIN BLUMUND.

BUT THAT DECISION WAS PROVEN CORRECT IN THE END.

SO YOU CHOSE TEMPEST OVER THE WESTERN HOLY CHURCH AS A SURVIVAL STRATEGY.

IS THAT CORRECT?

I SEE...

AND THAT IS WHY.

YOU MAY SAY THAT, GAZEL...

I APOLOGIZE FOR MY QUESTION, FUZE.

BUT NOW I FEEL THAT I UNDERSTAND.

...BUT FORMING OFFICIAL TIES WITH A COUNTRY OF MONSTERS IS NOT SUCH A SIMPLE MATTER.

THAT WAS NEEDLESSLY CUNNING, ERALD. YOU NEED NOT TEST A SMALL COUNTRY WHEN I TRUST RIMURU.

THAT SHOULD BE ENOUGH TO VOUCH FOR HIM.

...BUT BEFORE I ANSWER THAT QUESTION, I HAVE ONE MORE FOR RIMURU HIMSELF.

I HAVE MY OWN CONCLU-SION...

AND?

HAVE YOU MADE A DECISION?

Eren, dear, this is important...

I DO FEEL SORRY FOR HIM, SO I'LL JUST RESET THE TONE HERE.

SHHH!

COME ON, DAD! STOP PLAYING COY AND JUST ANSWER HIM!!

UM, MISS, NOW'S NOT THE TIME!

SO MUCH FOR THE DUKE'S DIGNITY.

WHAT WAS THAT?

I'M READY FOR YOUR QUESTION, ERALD.

THE DEMON LORD'S SPIRIT!

I ASK YOU, DEMON LORD RIMURU...

GULP

I SEE— IT IS A TREMENDOUS WEIGHT...

A LAND THAT IS BOUNTIFUL AND COMFORTABLE, WHERE ALL ARE HAPPY.

I WANT TO CREATE A WORLD...

...THAT IS EASY TO LIVE IN, ACCORDING TO MY DESIRES.

...I DON'T EXPECT IT TO BE THAT SIMPLE.

OF COURSE...

OF COURSE.

DO YOU *REALLY* THINK YOU CAN MAKE THIS HAPPEN?!

Y-YOU SPEAK OF DREAMS AND FANCIES, SIR...

I'M NOT INTERESTED IN POWER FOR POWER'S SAKE.

IT'S WHY THIS POWER EXISTS.

IDEALS WITHOUT STRENGTH ARE JUST IDLE DAYDREAMS. STRENGTH WITHOUT IDEALS IS JUST EMPTY FORCE.

HA... HA HA HA.

I WAS RIGHT! THIS *IS* DELIGHTFUL!

Daddy...

HA HA HA HA HA HA HA HA!

NO WONDER EREN TOOK TO HIM.

I FEEL AS THOUGH I UNDERSTAND HOW YOU WERE ABLE TO AWAKEN.

...I SEEK DIPLOMATIC RELATIONS WITH THE JURA TEMPEST FEDERATION.

PARDON MY INSO-LENCE.

AS AN ENVOY OF THE SORCEROUS DYNASTY OF THALION...

I WAS HOPING THAT WE COULD MAINTAIN GOOD RELATIONS.

I CERTAINLY ACCEPT.

177

I WAS TRYING TO BE MORE DEMON LORD-ISH. MAYBE I TOOK IT TOO FAR.

I'M SORRY, ER... LORD ERALD?

YOU KNEW YOU WERE JOINING THE MONSTERS' SIDE FROM THE START, YOU SCHEMER.

BUT THE LAST ANSWER TOLD ME HIS NATURE AS A DEMON LORD.

WITH THE STORM DRAGON INVOLVED, HOSTILITY WAS NEVER AN OPTION.

I WAS NOT EXPECTING TO BE INTIMIDATED ON A FIRST-NAME BASIS, HOWEVER.

Sorry...

BUT IN OFFICIAL TALKS, I WOULD APPRECIATE MY NAME AND TITLE.

IN PERSONAL CONVERSATION, JUST ERALD IS FINE.

178

YOU SHOULD DO IT MORE OFTEN.

THAT DEMON-STRATION WAS VERY EFFECTIVE.

I APPRE-CIATE YOUR ADVICE, DUKE ERALD.

I'm happy for you, Your Highness.

sniff sniff

Eren?!

You're the best, Dad!

ANOTHER HUMAN NATION HAS COME TO ACCEPT US.

THE SORCEROUS DYNASTY OF THALION.

I'll bring out some drinks.

Thanks.

LET'S HAVE A LITTLE BREAK.

A YOUNG MONSTER IS CLAIMING THE TITLE OF DEMON LORD?

WITH LADY MILIM AND LADY FREY AS SECONDS.

BY LORD CLAYMAN.

YES. AND THAT IS WHY AN ASSEMBLY OF THE WALPUR-GIS COUNCIL WAS PROPOSED.

I'LL NEVER UNDERSTAND HOW THAT IDIOT THINKS.

MILIM ...

Reincarnate
in Volume 17?

→YES

NO

Veldora's Slime Observation Journal
~CONCLUSION~

Veldora's Slime Observation Journal
~CONCLUSION~

◆THE UNLEASHED◆

At last, this day has come.

With great anticipation, I waited for Rimuru to liberate me. He seems to be headed somewhere—I can only assume it is where the process will begin.

Along the way, he promoted Gabiru to the position of officer, to much rejoicing—but I feel that my joy is greater.

"You seem very happy, Master Veldora."

"Kwa ha ha ha! Can you tell, Ifrit?"

"Well, of course. Anyone could, if they saw how restless you were."

Well, yes. Naturally, they would know.

At long last, I am going to be free from this vexatious Unlimited Imprisonment. What joy could be greater than that?

What should I do when I am free? Rimuru seems bent on striking at this Demon Lord Clayman, so it might be fun if I went and gave that Clayman a good wallop.

"Just a word of warning, Master Veldora..."

"Hmm? What?"

"I think it would be good if you did not take matters into your own hands."

"Ohhh?"

"I'm going to be very frank with you, because I don't think you're aware, but when you act on assumptions, it only causes problems for everyone else!!" Ifrit stated, much more firmly than usual.

"Have I ever caused a single problem for you, Ifrit?"

"Whaaat?!"

"Hmm?"

"...I'm sorry. I was so shocked, I completely forgot to answer your question."

"Oh, really?"

"I can't believe you're looking at me like you have no idea what I'm talking about. Oh, whatever. There are plenty of things I could say to you, but my issues aren't important right now. Think back on everything Lord Rimuru has done. Whenever he was going to do something significant, he always consulted with his companions, didn't he?"

"That is true. Rimuru is very careful, always mindful of others—"

"That! That's it, Master Veldora!"

"Hmm?"

"You just noticed something very important!"

Ahh, I noticed it, did I? That doesn't surprise me. When one is as wise as me, one is constantly noticing things.

"Continue," I bade Ifrit, waiting for the answer in a pleasant mood.

"What I mean is that being mindful of others at all times is very important!!"

"Ah, I see. So it was exactly what I said."

"Y-yes. Right. So just, listen to what people say, is my point."

"Indeed."

In fact, I doubt that Rimuru has any followers who are as mindful as I.

Shion? Not even close. Even after experiencing death, it has not changed her nature much.

Gobta is always getting hurt because he says one thing too many. I would never make such a mistake, so clearly Ifrit is worrying over nothing.

Geld has his good points, but he is too passive. Silence is golden, but sometimes one must speak up for oneself.

Shuna gets full marks for mindfulness, but she lacks strength.

Benimaru is fairly good in all categories, but it seems to me that he still overly relies upon Rimuru to tell him what to do.

So yes, I am the only one who can stand side by side with Rimuru.

"It's true that you are very powerful, Master Veldora..."

"Yes!"

"But you stand out."

"I suppose!"

"That wasn't a compliment. My point is, rather than agreeing with me, maybe you should be aware of that and take steps to fix it!"

"What?"

"You weren't thinking of sneaking off and dealing with Demon Lord Clayman all on your own, were you?"

W-w-what?!

Yes, I was thinking that. Was that a bad idea?

"I-I wasn't thinking that. Why do you ask?"

"Really?"

"Of course!"

I must push past this challenge. I know that if I fold here, I admit defeat.

"Well, that's good to hear. Just keep this in mind. If you want to stand at Lord Rimuru's side as his friend, then anything that you do will be blamed on Rimuru. There is a phrase called 'unwelcome favors.' It means that things you do for another person meant to be helpful may only harm the other person. Because you are so powerful, Master, you must consult with your companions before you do anything."

"Ah, I see..."

"You wouldn't want Lord Rimuru to be upset with you, would you?"

"I would cry."

"Then don't be careless, and strive to always be certain of what to do, before you do it. Be careful, be thoughtful, be mindful! You must promise!"

"Mm! I shall!" I said forcefully, completing our pact.

—And then, the moment arrived...—

"I'm going to let you out now, Veldora," I heard Rimuru say.

I replied with a great laugh. I had resigned myself to a hundred-year wait. Instead, my liberation has come far sooner.

And now that I, the mightiest being alive, am back, there is nothing to fear. Now I can look forward to a life of helping out Rimuru and being celebrated for my accomplishments.

Or at least, I should have been...

I do not understand.

This is not what I expected.

I was anticipating a bracing, moving reunion. Like, Veldora, you're the best!! But Rimuru is treating this like an ordinary occurrence.

I feel as though I've tripped on my very first step.

I was spying on Rimuru's life while on the inside, but I knew that it would be awkward to admit this, so I put every effort into fooling him during our conversation, but it seems that we are not quite seeing eye to eye.

However, I still have my trump card to play. If I show him this trick, he is certain to think better of me.

"Oh! Ohhh! My Unique Skill 'Inquirer' turned into the Ultimate Skill 'Faust'!! This power will help me reach the ultimate truth, the very desire of my boundless curiosity!!"

Perfect!

I waited for the right moment, and dropped the line I'd been practicing for so long.

And yet—!

"Oh, yeah. Wow. Amazing."

I can't help but feel that he just blew me off.

Huh? What does this mean? It left me at a loss, which is quite understandable.

Luckily, I received a present so wonderful that it eliminated all thought of this shocking occurrence.

Rimuru arranged for an augmented body double to be my flesh. It feels very familiar, perhaps because the magicules are very similar. This is probably because I spent so much time in Rimuru's stomach, such that we shared our magicules with one another. Because these mutual magicules exist in both of our bodies, I did not experience any rejection symptoms.

This was an unexpected gift—or was it all according to plan?

......

Huh?

No response.

Normally I would receive an answer like, "Affirmative: I have designed it to withstand the tremendous presence of a dragon," but this time, there is nothing.

Ah, yes. Because I have returned to life, I no longer have the old connection to Raphael, that power of Rimuru's.

And naturally, there is no Ifrit here, either. That makes me lonely, and a little worried.

Careful, thoughtful, mindful.

That was my promise to Ifrit.

From now on, I will have to live up to Rimuru's expectations on my own. I chatted lightly with my old friend, hiding my concerns.

And then, on Rimuru's request, I began to practice controlling my aura.

◆SWIRLING PLOTS◆

This is harder than I thought!

The hope was that I would prove it to be a snap, earning the compliments of all, but I daresay I am actually struggling.

This is all the fault of my copious amounts of magical energy. Simply coming into contact with my aura would kill a weak human. Monsters have slightly more resistance, but even that resistance has its limits.

I don't need Rimuru to tell me that this is where I really need to put in the work.

But mastery is far off, in spite of my continued efforts. In fact, it feels as though my power is even vaster than before. I do not think I can contain this aura.

It's gotten to the point that the panic is causing my concentration to lapse. The third day of practice is soon to end, and I haven't even found a clue to get started. I desperately need a hint.

Just at that moment!

"Question: Can you hear me? YES / NO"

I heard a familiar voice.

"Oh, is that you, Raphael? Have you come rushing to my side in this, my moment of need?!"

"Negative. I have only spoken to you to confirm the establishment of a Soul Corridor between Master and the individual Veldora—"

"You're lying."

I was aware that Rimuru was condensing and improving his skills. Knowing how excellent Raphael is at its job, I knew that it was utilizing the last remnants of my ability to assess and analyze.

But that would mean the Soul Corridor was established a long time ago. The fact that it chose now to speak to me must be a sign that it wants to help me.

"...Affirmative. Sadly, it is true."

Of course it is!

"Then as a reward for guessing correctly, you must tell me the way to properly control my aura."

"Affirmative. Please use this as reference."

Oh! The mental image of the technique went straight from Raphael into my head. I presume this is thanks to the Soul Corridor, but it is extremely useful. The idea simply sprang into my mind, like *ding!*

After all, it perfectly matched with the holy manga texts that I read.

Based on this reference, it would seem that I should resort to the "Veldora-style Killing Arts" that I practiced so much. And that should make this quite simple.

"Report: Decrease in aura detected from the individual Veldora."

Good, good.

If I can limit the external leaking to this level, I can prevent doing damage to the weaklings.

The real problem will be how long my patience can last, but I am currently low on fuel anyway, so I should be fine for now. If I have trouble, I'm sure Rimuru will handle things, so that settles this problem.

"Have you confirmed all of your skills, Rimuru?"

"Yeah. You've learned how to control your aura, I see," said Rimuru. His compliment made me feel very good.

"Kwaa ha ha ha ha! Such a task is no challenge for me at all!"

Of course, I got the hint from Raphael, but that does not need to be said here.

At any rate, my preparations are complete. At last, the time has come for me to be introduced to Rimuru's companions.
I am feeling a little nervous. Will they properly fawn over my greatness?

I put together a very detailed plan with Ifrit, but now I am alone. It might be the loneliest I have ever felt in my very long life.

"Sigh. I am doing you a major favor. I have connected the individuals Veldora and Ifrit via the Soul Corridor. This will make Thought Communication possible, so you should confer whenever needed."

My word!

This is Raphael at its best, living up to Rimuru's reputation.

Is this what they call a tsundere?

"Negative: That is incorrect."

Kwaa ha ha ha! Don't be so humble!

Were you keeping an eye out for me? You have my word that your kindness will not be wasted.

"Hello, Ifrit? Can you hear me?"

"I can hear you. Are you already feeling lonely on the third day?"

"F-fool! Of course I am not!! Raphael was worried that you might be lonely, so I took it upon myself to speak to you."

"Okay, sure. We can say that's what's going on."

What is this? Ifrit seems...strangely unconcerned with me?

"Why aren't you feeling lonely, then?"

"Well, Raphael made it possible for me to see the outside world, so I haven't been bored in here."

Gya-wha?!

That is not fair!

I want to complain, but then again, I was sneaking peeks at what Rimuru was doing, so I cannot speak too forcefully...

"But if I'm being honest, I am heartened. I was afraid that you would simply forget all about me, Master Veldora."

"Ifrit..."

I was at a loss for words.

That's right. Ifrit was left behind in that prison-like stomach all alone. I was only concerned with my own affairs, and never stopped to consider Ifrit's solitude.

"I promise you this, Ifrit. I will ensure that you are liberated from that place."

"Ha ha ha, then I'll look forward to that day."

"Good! Until then, work hard under Raphael's tutelage."

"Um, that may not be your problem anymore, Master Veldora, but it's a terrible trial for me—"

"Kwaaaa ha ha ha! Kwaaaaa ha ha ha haaa!!"

"This isn't funny!"

Have no fear, Ifrit. Like Rimuru, I always keep my promises. It will not take long for this promise to be fulfilled.

"May our relationship be long and prosperous."

"Yes, of course! After all, if I don't keep an eye on you, Master, I'm afraid I'll be too worried to focus on my training."

Ifrit has developed quite the saucy tongue. While it might be rude, his growth pleases me.

Plus, over the course of our conversation, I found that my fears had melted away.

Rimuru's companions have gathered outside the cave and are squalling about something or other, but I am in fine form. I am ready to greet them as his friend.

And this is the historic first step of my new, delightful adventure!

The end.

I have been recording this "Slime Observation Journal" since Rimuru and I first met, and I think that for now, I shall be laying down my pen.

I will be too busy to write this in the days ahead, no doubt because my own exploits will take center stage.

Of course, I will continue to observe Rimuru, so if the opportunity should arise, I might deliver some comments of my own again. If that should happen, you will have the double gift of my thoughts and my actions together.

Be well, my readers.

Heh heh heh.

Kwaa ha ha ha!

Kwaaaaaa ha ha ha ha ha!!

Until the day we meet again.

To be reincarnated in Volume 17!

LIST OF ACKNOWLEDGMENTS

AUTHOR:
Fuse-sensei

CHARACTER DESIGN:
Mitz Vah-sensei

ASSISTANTS:
Muraichi-san
Daiki Haraguchi-san
Masashi Kiritani-sensei
Taku Arao-sensei

Everyone at the editorial department

congrats on your series!

AND YOU!!

I've lost some weight.

GOLDEN YELLOW WOULD WORK, TOO

WHICH OF THESE COULD VELDORA WEAR...?

I CAN'T LET HIM BE HALF-NAKED IN FRONT OF FOREIGN DIGNITARIES.

I DO NOT KNOW THE NAME.

OH? WHAT IS IT?

Very cool ones

I KNOW WHAT CLOTHES I WISH TO WEAR, RIMURU.

AND THE HEM LOOKS LIKE THIS...

YES. YOU SEE, THE COLLAR GOES LIKE THIS.

SWISH! SWISH!

CAN YOU DRAW IT FOR ME, THEN?

BA BAM!!

WHAT WERE DOING THE WHOLE TIME YOU WERE IN MY STOMACH?

THERE! THAT IS BASICALLY WHAT IT LOOKS LIKE!

Sticky bun.

Filled with steaming slime

TRANSLATION
NOTES

ALL WHO DEFY ME...

The precise wording of Veldora's line here appears to be unique, and is not obviously based on any particular line from manga and anime. But it is reminiscent of various villains and bad boys from manga history. In particular, "All who defy me get the death penalty!" is a notable line from the bully character Gian (Big G) from *Doraemon*, whose self-important and selfish attitude is most definitely shared with Veldora.

DETECTIVE DOYLE

MANGA: Detective Doyle

This fictional manga, due to the name reference (Conan Arthur Doyle, writer of *Sherlock Holmes*) and cover design, is clearly a play on the popular detective manga, *Detective Conan (Case Closed)*.

THE KINDAICHI CASE!!

A parody of the famous mystery manga series *The Kindaichi Case Files*, a popular and long-running series that has gone through several permutations since it began in the early 1990s. As a lengthy and successful murder-mystery series starting around the same time, it has long had a friendly rivalry with Detective Conan. The titular character Hajime Kindaichi is considered to be a genius, as Veldora alludes to on page 157.

VELDORA'S OUTFIT

The "cool" clothing that Veldora wants to wear is essentially Saiyan battle armor from *Dragon Ball Z*, another hint at what he has been reading while stuck in Rimuru's stomach with nothing else to do.

That
Time I Got
Reincarnated
as a
Slime

WATCH ON crunchyroll

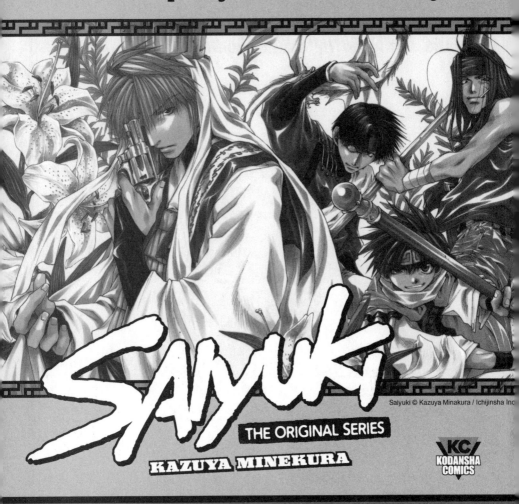

Young characters and steampunk setting, like *Howl's Moving Castle* and *Battle Angel Alita*

Beyond the Clouds © 2018 Nicke / Ki-oon

A boy with a talent for machines and a mysterious girl whose wings he's fixed will take you beyond the clouds! In the tradition of the high-flying, resonant adventure stories of Studio Ghibli comes a gorgeous tale about the longing of young hearts for adventure and friendship!

Knight of the Ice ©Yayoi Ogawa/Kodansha Ltd.

SKATING THRILLS AND ICY CHILLS WITH THIS NEW TINGLY ROMANCE SERIES!

A rom-com on ice, perfect for fans of *Princess Jellyfish* and *Wotakoi*. Kokoro is the talk of the figure-skating world, winning trophies and hearts. But little do they know... he's actually a huge nerd! From the beloved creator of *You're My Pet* (*Tramps Like Us*).

Chitose is a serious young woman, working for the health magazine *SASSO*. Or at least, she would be, if she wasn't constantly getting distracted by her childhood friend, international figure skating star Kokoro Kijinami! In the public eye and on the ice, Kokoro is a gallant, flawless knight, but behind his glittery costumes and breathtaking spins lies a secret: He's actually a hopelessly romantic otaku, who can only land his quad jumps when Chitose is on hand to recite a spell from his favorite magical girl anime!

KC KODANSHA COMICS

A Kodansha Comics Trade Paperback Original
That Time I Got Reincarnated as a Slime 16 copyright © 2020 Fuse / Taiki Kawakami
English translation copyright © 2021 Fuse / Taiki Kawakami

Published in the United States by Kodansha Comics, an imprint of
Kodansha USA Publishing, LLC, New York.

Publication rights for this English edition arranged through
Kodansha Ltd., Tokyo.

First published in Japan in 2020 by Kodansha Ltd., Tokyo
as *Tensei Shitara Suraimu Datta Ken*, volume 16.

ISBN 978-1-64651-169-3

Original cover design by Saya Takagi (RedRooster)

Printed in the United States of America.

www.kodansha.us

9 8 7 6 5 4 3 2 1
Translation: Stephen Paul
Lettering: Evan Hayden
Editing: Vanessa Tenazas
Kodansha Comics edition cover design by Phil Balsman

Publisher: Kiichiro Sugawara

Director of publishing services: Ben Applegate
Associate director of operations: Stephen Pakula
Publishing services managing editorial: Alanna Ruse, Madison Salters
Assistant production manager: Emi Lotto, Angela Zurlo